THE HERITAGE COLLECTION

MWENE MUTAPA

The Forgotten African Kingdom

Letitia deGraft Okyere

Illustrated by Masum Ahmed

Mwene Mutapa: The Forgotten African Kingdom

Copyright © 2024 by Letitia deGraft Okyere

Illustrator: Masum Ahmed

Layout designer: Nassim Sarkar

Library of Congress Control Number: 2023901314

All rights reserved.

No part of this publication may be reproduced, stored in a retrieval system, a database, and/or published in any form or by any means, electronic, mechanical, photocopying, recording or otherwise, without the prior written permission of the publisher.

ISBN 978-1-956776-16-4 hardcover
ISBN 978-1-956776-17-1 ebook

Published by Lion's Historian Press
https://www.lionshistorian.net/

For

Angelina, John, and Alec

Brief Introduction

Before Mwene Mutapa

The territory between the Zambezi and Limpopo rivers, bordered on the east by the Indian Ocean, has been home to Shona-speaking people for centuries. Historians write that the Shona Kingdom of Zimbabwe existed in that region, as far back as the 1100s. Ancient Zimbabwe was known for its city, Great Zimbabwe.

Great Zimbabwe, located around Masvingo in southeastern modern Zimbabwe, was home to the local monarch and a place of political power. An active center for trade, the Shona gave gold and ivory in exchange for items such as glass beads and Chinese pottery. Its unique stone structures show that Great Zimbabwe's masons joined stone blocks without mortar. Visitors to the area today will find some two hundred stone ruins, telling of the ancient builder's skill in Africa. The Great Enclosure, an example of the ruins, stands with walls thirty-six feet high.

It is believed that Great Zimbabwe fell because the land could no longer support its population. Over time, as Great Zimbabwe lost its significance, Mwene Mutapa rose to become a leading nation in Southeast Africa.

Contents

Chapter 1: Mwene Mutapa 1
Chapter 2: Nyatsimba Mutota 3
Chapter 3: System of Governance 5
Chapter 4: Living in the Kingdom 7
Chapter 5: Wealth Through Trade 9
Chapter 6: Arrival of the Portuguese 11
Chapter 7: The King Converts to Christianity 13
Chapter 8: The Priest is Sentenced 15
Chapter 9: The Portuguese Plan Punishment 17
Chapter 10: Mwene Mutapa Begins to Fall 19
Chapter 11: Portuguese Influence Grows 21
Chapter 12: Invasion by the Changamire 23
Chapter 13: Mwene Mutapa Falls 25
Chapter 14: Reasons for Mwene Mutapa's Decline 27
Epilogue: Remnants of Mwene Mutapa 29
Glossary 31
Quiz 33
Word Puzzle 35
References 37
Fun Fact About the Zambezi River 39
Other Books in the Heritage Collection 41

Chapter 1

Mwene Mutapa

Oral Shona tradition tells us that in the first half of the 1400s, Great Zimbabwe began to fall. The land was overused and no longer produced crops. Miners could not find gold in its mines. A warrior from Great Zimbabwe traveled north, about 350 miles, in search of new natural resources. The warrior found fertile land with access to important trading posts along the Zambezi River. Soon, this warrior overpowered the Shona people who lived there, and established the Kingdom of Mwene Mutapa.

This warrior was Nyatsimba Mutota, the first king of the new state, Mwene Mutapa. Many from Great Zimbabwe and other neighboring states followed Nyatsimba Mutota and settled in the area. By 1450, Mwene Mutapa had become the most important Shona state in southeastern Africa.

In modern times, Mwene Mutapa is said to have covered parts of Mozambique, Zimbabwe, and Zambia. However, some historians suggest that at its height, Mwene Mutapa included parts of what is now Angola and Tanzania and extended to the Indian Ocean.

Chapter 2

Nyatsimba Mutota

The title for the kingdom's leader was *mwene*, meaning conquering lord or king, and *mutapa*, meaning conquered land. With time, the kingdom came to be known as Mwene Mutapa, after the founding leader, as he conquered lands. Mwene Mutapa is sometimes written as *Munhumutapa*. Portuguese traders, unable to pronounce Munhumutapa, corrupted the name to Monomotapa.

The founding leader, Mwene Nyatsimba Mutota, used a decorated hoe with an ivory handle as his symbol of authority. Often, as part of his regalia, he carried a spear made from ivory and gold. Ivory indicated that he was the king of a peaceful nation, and the gold told of Mwene Mutapa's mines. Nyatsimba Mutota built a capital city protected by a wooden wall and recruited young men to train as guards, who later became soldiers. Builders in Mwene Mutapa did not continue the Great Zimbabwe tradition of stone construction.

Matope Nyanhehwe succeeded Nyatsimba Mutota and ruled for thirty years, expanding the kingdom's territory. Matope Nyanhehwe's warriors captured lands to the south and east, including coastal states. The newly acquired states were required to pay tributes to the king of Mwene Mutapa.

Chapter 3

System of Governance

Mwene Mutapa had a strong army for defeating neighboring states and maintaining peace at home. The king ruled over the different parts of the state through a three-layered system. The capital city was on top of this system of governance, then provinces, with villages on the lowest level. The king was assisted by administrators and governors who ruled over provinces like judges. To foster loyalty, the king regularly gave gifts to his administrators and governors, and these, in turn, sent their sons to the king's court, the *dzimbahwe*, to serve as pages.

The citizens had respect for the king because of his role as the leader of the state's religion. The citizens gave the king offerings of cattle and other items to show their devotion. They were so interested in the king's daily activities that they developed a method for sharing news about him. Stories of the king's pursuits traveled far and wide by this informal process.

The king allowed his subjects some freedom, helping to create harmony and stability in society. Other states then voluntarily agreed to join Mwene Mutapa. To strengthen Mwene Mutapa's bond with these states, the king offered their leaders seats on his council. Mwene Mutapa united several groups in southern Africa using diplomacy, without always having to declare war.

Chapter 4

Living in the Kingdom

The people of Mwene Mutapa farmed for a living, producing millet, beans, cowpeas, bananas, and sorghum. In some provinces, hired laborers cultivated the land. Some citizens reared cattle, and successful ranchers increased their social and political power.

The Shona wove fabrics on looms resting close to the ground, including *Machira* from local cotton. The use of Machira was restricted to those with influence in society. The fabric was draped on the king's throne as a sign of his authority, worn by the wealthy like governors and land owners, and presented to priests as an offering. The fabric is still used by some Shona groups. Mwene Mutapa had rich gold mines. It is believed that the Shona of Mwene Mutapa discovered all the gold mines in present-day Zimbabwe. When European traders and settlers arrived in Mwene Mutapa, they found that the Shona had developed a mining process.

The conquest of other states gave Mwene Mutapa access to copper and ivory. As a result, a class of skilled blacksmiths grew. The blacksmiths made weapons for war, tools for farming, and spears for hunting game like elephants. Mwene Mutapa's craftsmen smelted iron, making wired beads from copper and metal artifacts depicting their culture. They made delicate jewelry like bracelets, anklets, and other decorative ornaments worn by the women.

Chapter 5

Wealth Through Trade

Mwene Mutapa built markets along the Zambezi River, trading across the Indian Ocean. The citizens of Mwene Mutapa were free to produce and sell items centered around family. Family units mined gold, made iron and copper crafts, farmed and sold produce, or were game hunters who traded ivory.

Although the king did not place limits on production and trade in the provinces, there was a system of sales taxes. There were levies on gold mining profits based on weight. For farmers, seven days out of every thirty days' worth of produce belonged to the kingdom. When citizens refused to pay taxes, the army enforced payment. Mwene Mutapa had measures and standards to ensure fairness. Administrators managed the quantity of produce transported to the markets to keep a check on prices. Craftsmen were so skilled they produced iron of a higher quality than Portuguese iron. In addition, as African ivory is easier to carve than Indian ivory, it earned higher profits.

Trading partners included India, China, Arabia, Indonesia, and later, Portugal. As Arab traders played an important role, the king had a special representative at his court to resolve disputes. Mwene Mutapa traded gold and farm produce in exchange for blue and white Chinese porcelain and beads, Indian silks and spices, Indonesian livestock, and Portuguese luxury items. There was trade with African coastal communities in the east, like Sofala and Kilwa, and in the south, beyond the Limpopo River. Mwene Mutapa's trade and taxation system made the kingdom rich and powerful.

Chapter 6

Arrival of the Portuguese

Mwene Mutapa's abundance of natural wealth, such as gold and ivory, caused the Portuguese to believe it was the ancient city of Ophir. The Bible recorded that every three years, King Solomon of ancient Israel, received shipments of silver, gold, pearls, ivory, peacocks, and other luxury items from Ophir.

After landing in Elmina on the west coast of Africa in 1471, the Portuguese traveled southeast in search of Ophir. The Portuguese reached the port of Sofala now in Mozambique around 1505 and traveled over a thousand miles north to Kilwa, a trading center. Kilwa is now in Tanzania. They found a profitable trade pattern between Arabs, Mwene Mutapa and its provinces, and India.

The Portuguese attacked towns on the southeastern coast, beginning with Kilwa. They established trading forts at Sofala and Kilwa and gained access to the gold trade. Portugal's gold and ivory shipments went to Goa in India, its headquarters along the eastern trading zone. The Portuguese quickly grew inpatient with the restricted role in the gold trade and sought to travel inland, to Mwene Mutapa. There, still thought by some Europeans to be Ophir, they would seize the kingdom's gold mines. However, the Mwene Mutapa king held back Portuguese efforts to move freely across the kingdom. When the Portuguese failed to pay required taxes, the Mwene Mutapa king took possession of Portuguese assets.

Chapter 7

The King Converts to Christianity

King Neshangwe ruled from 1530 to 1550 and allowed the Portuguese to establish a trade mission by 1540. The Portuguese could not fully monitor the trade along the eastern African coast unless they established a base further inside the region. The Portuguese compensated Mwene Mutapa with interest payments and tributes. Governors of Portuguese fortresses in what is now Mozambique provided 3,000 cruzados worth of cloth and beads to Mwene Mutapa's king every three years in exchange for safe passage through the kingdom.

The Portuguese sent a priest to Mwene Mutapa to convert the king, hoping that it would give them an additional trade advantage. Father Dom Goncalo da Silveira visited the capital city of Masapa in 1561 during King Mupunzagutu's reign. Dom da Silveira made progress by baptizing King Mupunzagutu, his mother, and many members of the royal household.

This conversion was against Mwene Mutapa's religious traditions. It made the council of elders angry; they never wanted the Portuguese in Mwene Mutapa in the first place. The elders believed the Portuguese planned to rule over them. Arab traders, on the other hand, were concerned about possible future limits on their gold trade. It was clear that Dom da Silveira was strengthening his influence over the king and who got access to Mwene Mutapa's gold mines.

Chapter 8

The Priest is Sentenced

Mwene Mutapa's council of elders and Arab traders reminded the king of Portugal's plans to overpower the kingdom. They pointed to the Portuguese use of more advanced weapons at the trading ports of Sofala and Kilwa. Also, during this time, there was a sense of insecurity in Mwene Mutapa. The perceived threat from the Portuguese and their past use of advanced weapons in the region, coupled with internal unrest, made the king and the citizens nervous. The Mwene Mutapa king saw the need to shield his people by building up the state's defenses. The king ordered the installation of protective walls and stockades.

Even though the king strengthened Mwene Mutapa's defense system, concerns about the Portuguese presence continued. All those who opposed the Portuguese in Mwene Mutapa insisted that the king demand Dom da Silveira's departure. Dom da Silveira ignored the warning messages delivered to his home. The priest was confident his relationship with the king gave him enough protection.

The Mwene Mutapa council held a meeting when Dom da Silveira remained in the kingdom. Council members reviewed the evidence piled against Dom da Silveira and sentenced the priest to death. The king summoned a second council meeting, hoping to have the decision reversed with a vow to return the priest to Portugal. The death sentence was upheld, and Dom Goncalo da Silveira was executed as a traitor.

Chapter 9

The Portuguese Plan Punishment

Following da Silveira's death, Mwene Mutapa continued to resist Portuguese attempts to interfere with its gold and ivory trade. So, the Portuguese decided to punish the kingdom for the priest's death. The Portuguese believed that the process of inflicting punishment would be a vehicle for taking control over Mwene Mutapa's trade activities, especially its gold mines.

The Portuguese army led by Barreto in 1568 got as far as the Zambezi River. They were defeated by the locals and suffered death from diseases. The Portuguese returned to their base, intermarried with the natives, and created estate holders known as the prazeiros. Another expedition led by Homem made it to Mwene Mutapa but withdrew to the coast. Homem discovered gold mining was difficult work.

Despite these and other threats from the Portuguese, Mwene Mutapa retained its position and put a heavy tax on all imported goods and Portuguese estate holders. In the late 1500s, the Mwene Mutapa king made a trade deal with the Portuguese, an agreement of value to both sides. Thus, through to the close of the 1500s, the Mwene Mutapa king continued to keep his kingdom unified, restricting access to its markets and trade routes. However, at the turn of the new century, this would change.

Chapter 10

Mwene Mutapa Begins to Fall

By the early 1600s, the kingdom faced many problems. Different groups within Mwene Mutapa claimed rights to the throne, and each side built an alliance with the Portuguese to help defeat its rival. Mwene Mutapa's acquired territories – Kiteve, Madanda, and Manyi – recognized the decreasing power of the king and stopped paying tribute as vassals, adding to the uncertainty.

Gatsi Rusere, the Mwene Mutapa king who reigned for three decades until about 1623, sought support from the Portuguese. Gatsi Rusere was so desperate to retain power that he gave the Portuguese mining rights. This grant allowed the Portuguese to challenge Mwene Mutapa's dominance over the gold trade and tension in Mwene Mutapa increased.

In the meanwhile, the neighboring Rozwi Kingdom, led by kings known as Changamire, grew more powerful. Rozwi was southwest of Mwene Mutapa, in present-day Zimbabwe. Changamire Dombo was a cattle herder who became the leader of the Rozwi Kingdom, another state emerging out of the Great Zimbabwe region. Dombo built a strong army used to push the Portuguese out of the area and crush neighboring kingdoms.

Chapter 11

Portuguese Influence Grows

The throne passed to Nyambo Kapararidze, Gatsi Rusere's son. Nyambo Kapararidze went to war against the Portuguese when they changed the rules on tribute payments. Nyambo Kapararidze planned to remove the Portuguese from the region. The Mwene Mutapa king defeated hundreds of Portuguese soldiers and thousands of their African fighters. It was the worst defeat the Portuguese had seen in Southeast Africa. The Portuguese responded with force and replaced Nyambo Kapararidze with his uncle, Mavura Mhande Felipe. Mavura had converted to Christianity and thus was favored by the Portuguese.

Mavura Mhande signed a treaty with the Portuguese in 1629, allowing the prazeiros to build fortified settlements, making Mwene Mutapa a subject of Portugal. It abolished taxes paid by the Portuguese to Mwene Mutapa. The Portuguese had taken slaves who were made to farm the lands acquired. Mavura Mhande hoped that the treaty would keep him on the throne, but it did not, for several reasons. First, Mavura was not liked because he was controlled by the Portuguese. Second, the use of Africans by the Portuguese as slaves caused anger. Third, Mavura rejected his traditional religion and openly practiced his new Christian faith. Fourth, the Portuguese expansion of trade and political influence led to armed internal clashes, causing many in Mwene Mutapa to flee to the Rozwi Kingdom for refuge.

Chapter 12

Invasion by the Changamire

Decades later, Mwene Mutapa continued to suffer internal conflict from opposing groups. At the same time, Mwene Mutapa faced threats from the Rozwi Kingdom while the Portuguese tried to use their new position to acquire more lands. Mavura Mhande Felipe died around 1652, and after short reigns by kings influenced by the Portuguese, Mukombwe ascended the throne in 1663. King Mukombwe did not keep a friendly relationship with the Portuguese as he sought to take back control of his kingdom and the lands lost.

By 1680, the Rozwi Kingdom was in a position to overpower King Mukombwe and the Portuguese in Mwene Mutapa. Vassal states had broken away from Mwene Mutapa. The state's wealth from trading had decreased. In 1684, Changamire Dombo attacked a Portuguese stronghold in Mwene Mutapa and weakened their status. King Mukombwe thought he could take advantage of the situation to regain Mwene Mutapa's lost status. King Mukombwe's plan failed. His forces sent to Rozwi were defeated by Changamire Dombo's warriors returning from their battle with the Portuguese. The Rozwi Kingdom then gained a foothold in Mwene Mutapa.

Chapter 13

Mwene Mutapa Falls

King Mukombwe died almost ten years later, in 1692, and the kingdom fell into further chaos. The Portuguese desired to place Mukombwe's son on the throne. However, according to Shona tradition, Nyakaunembire, Mukombwe's brother, was the rightful heir. Nyakaunembire went to Changamire Dombo for help, and he was only too happy to step in. Changamire Dombo's forces destroyed Portuguese markets and their trade in Mwene Mutapa. By 1695, Rozwi regulated the lucrative gold trade in the region, and the king of Mwene Mutapa had no real authority.

During the 1700s, succession disputes caused more unrest in Mwene Mutapa. Each king's death led to an internal war. Rival parties continued to seek help from either the Portuguese or Rozwi Changamire. Rozwi soon lost interest in Mwene Mutapa and the state gained its independence, but it was restricted to a smaller area. Mwene Mutapa was forced to move from the northern part of the Zimbabwe plateau it once occupied to the Zambezi lowlands, now Mozambique. Mwene Mutapa's place as the most powerful state was overtaken by the Rozwi Kingdom.

Chapter 14

Reasons for Mwene Mutapa's Decline

There are many reasons why Mwene Mutapa fell. The most damaging cause was the violent succession disputes. The fighting between opposing sides led to marked divisions that were difficult for the winning side to bridge. Thus, each king's quest to encourage loyalty among the people became more difficult. Smooth succession processes became a thing of the past. Another important reason for Mwene Mutapa's collapse stemmed from the Portuguese influence on who became king and how trade activities were decided at the king's court.

In addition, Mwene Mutapa's downfall was connected to its loss of control over the trade network. An increase in the number of markets managed by the Portuguese meant a decrease in taxes to the king's court. The 1629 treaty did not help Mwene Mutapa either; it enabled the Portuguese to deepen their power over the gold trade. Finally, the combination of all these factors discussed created a path for the Rozwi Kingdom to overpower and displace Mwene Mutapa's position in the region.

Epilogue

Remnants of Mwene Mutapa

Despite Mwene Mutapa's collapse, it remains an example of an organized and flourishing state in Southeast Africa, one that existed before the arrival of European traders and settlers. Mwene Mutapa provided a stable environment for the Shona people in the region and encouraged trading by individuals. The history of Mwene Mutapa is significant because, for many years, it was believed that such societies only existed after European settlers arrived on the continent.

The people of Mwene Mutapa developed mining methods, and skilled craftsmen made artifacts and delicate ornaments from gold, copper, and iron. By 1506, Europeans discovered that Africans knew how to mine gold without relying on foreign methods. Trading activities were regulated by accepted measures. This ensured that standards applied to all exchanges. Administrators posted at the various markets monitored and enforced fair practices between buyers and sellers.

This Shona group was not completely wiped out. Those remaining formed a new kingdom in present-day Mozambique, said to have existed from 1803 to the early 1900s. Sometimes, this second Mwene Mutapa state is referred to as Karanga, with kings addressed as Mambo. The last king, Mambo Chioko, died in battle with the Portuguese.

Glossary

Great Zimbabwe	An ancient capital city built of stones without the use of mortar.
Changamire	The Changamire state, also known as Rozwi (or Rozvi), was founded in the late 1400s, southwest of Mwene Mutapa. It was in present-day Zimbabwe.
Mutota	King Mutota is believed to be the first ruler of Mwene Mutapa, by Shona oral tradition.
Prazos	Land grants to Portuguese settlers. Holders of these grants were called the prazeiros. This allowed the Portuguese crown to receive income from the land granted to its settlers in Africa.
Indian Ocean trade	The trade across the Indian Ocean allowed traders from as far as India, Persia, and Arabia to trade on the East African coast.
Kilwa	A former commercial center in what is now Tanzania. It had a lot of settlers from Arabia and Persia (now Iran) who went to the African coast to trade.

Sofala	Sofala is believed to have the oldest harbor in southern Africa, capable of holding one hundred ships. It is now in Mozambique and is no longer in operation.
Limpopo River	The Limpopo River begins in South Africa and travels through Mozambique before it empties into the Indian Ocean.
Cruzados	Historically, these were Portuguese gold or silver coins bearing the symbol of a cross.
Shona-speaking people	The Shona people are a Bantu ethnic group from southern Africa. Modern-day Zimbabwe has the largest group of Shona people.
Zambezi River	The Zambezi River flows from west to east in southern Africa. It empties into the Indian Ocean.

Quiz

1. What was the name of the first ruler of Mwene Mutapa?

    (a) Mavura
    (b) Mutota
    (c) Changamire
    (d) Chivere

2. Which ancient capital city is known for its stone buildings?

    (a) Sofala
    (b) Kilwa
    (c) Great Zimbabwe
    (d) Zambezi

3. What was the fabric woven by the people of Mwene Mutapa?

    (a) Kente
    (b) Kubaa
    (c) Machira
    (d) Kilim

4. **Which rising southern African state threatened Mwene Mutapa's place of power in the region?**
    (a) Manyinka
    (b) Zimbabwe
    (c) Teve
    (d) Rozwi

5. **What was the name of the priest sentenced to death?**
    (a) Dom da Silveira
    (b) Homem
    (c) Barreto
    (d) Dom da Costa

6. **Which king signed the 1629 treaty with the Portuguese?**
    (a) Gatsi Rusere
    (b) Nyambo Kapararidze
    (c) Nyatsimba Mutota
    (d) Mavura Mhande Felipe

Quiz Answers: BCCDAD

Word Puzzle

C	H	A	N	G	A	M	I	R	E	L	M	M	N
B	C	M	A	V	U	R	A	P	K	N	N	U	Y
U	W	H	P	L	L	Z	X	L	R	D	E	P	A
Z	I	M	B	A	B	W	E	M	Z	M	S	U	K
H	K	Z	A	M	B	E	Z	I	C	U	H	N	A
B	N	Y	A	T	S	I	M	B	A	K	A	Z	U
U	Y	C	B	R	K	X	Z	S	M	O	N	A	N
M	A	Q	Q	M	Y	P	W	Y	W	M	G	G	E
A	M	R	R	V	A	H	H	S	E	B	W	U	M
M	B	T	S	O	T	T	J	Y	N	W	E	T	B
B	O	S	T	L	Z	Y	O	W	E	E	M	U	I
O	N	Y	Y	N	B	W	S	P	Z	T	K	R	R
X	G	A	T	S	I	C	I	G	E	X	R	T	E
G	M	X	M	T	C	M	U	T	A	P	A	G	Y

NAMES, TITLES, AND KINGDOMS

1. **NYATSIMBA**
2. **MATOPE**
3. **NESHANGWE**
4. **ROZWI**
5. **CHANGAMIRE**
6. **GATSI**
7. **MUKOMBWE**
8. **MUTAPA**
9. **NYAKAUNEMBIRE**
10. **MAMBO**
11. **ZIMBABWE**
12. **MWENE**
13. **MUPUNZAGUTU**
14. **ZAMBEZI**
15. **MAVURA**

References

Manyanga, Munyaradzi, and Shadreck Chirikure, editors. *Archives, Objects, Places and Landscapes: Multidisciplinary Approaches to Decolonised Zimbabwean Pasts.* Langaa RPCIG, 2017. *JSTOR*, https://doi.org/10.2307/j.ctvh9vz54. Accessed 8 August, 2021.

Nicolaides, A. "Early Portuguese imperialism: using the Jesuits in the Mutapa Empire of Zimbabwe." *International Journal of Peace and Development Studies*, vol. 2, no. 4, April 2011, pp. 132-137.

Davy, Kenneth. "The Changamire Dombo: The Skills of an Emperor." *The Mirror - Undergraduate History Journal*, vol. 26, no. 1, Mar. 2006, pp. 196-11, https://ojs.lib.uwo.ca/index.php/westernumirror/article/view/15991. Accessed 20 December, 2023.

Huffman, T.N. "The Rise and Fall of Zimbabwe." *The Journal of African History*, vol. 13, no. 3, 1972, pp. 353-366.

Bhila, H.H.K. *The Manyika and the Portuguese 1575-1863.* 1971. University of London, PhD dissertation. *ProQuest*, search.proquest.com/openview/0e936dcd-d29ae733899f643c32b551dc/1?pq-origsite=gscholar&cbl=18750&diss=y.

Ranger, Terence O. *The Last Days of the Empire of Mwene Mutapa, 1898-1917.* Zimbabwe U, May 1963, https://ir.uz.ac.zw/bitstream/handle/10646/3200/Ranger_The_last_days_of_the_Empire_of_Mwene_Mutapa_%20%282%29.pdf?sequence=1&isAllowed=y. Accessed 24 August, 2021.

de Graft-Johnson, John Coleman. *African Glory: The Story of Vanished Negro Civilizations.* New York, Walker and Company, 1954.

de Graft-Johnson, John Coleman. "The Kingdom of Monomotapa." *Africana Quarterly Magazine,* vol. 1, no. 2, April 1949, pp. 5-6.

Fun Fact About the Zambezi River

The Zambezi flows from west to east across southern Africa into the Indian Ocean. Along the way, the Zambezi passes over a 335-foot fall the local Bantu people named *Mosi o Tunya* (The Smoke That Thunders) because of its roar and steam. In 1855, Scottish physician and explorer David Livingstone named it after Britain's Queen Victoria. Mosi o Tunya, commonly known as Victoria Falls, is almost twice as high and wide as Niagara Falls, along the border of the United States and Canada.

Other Books in the Heritage Collection

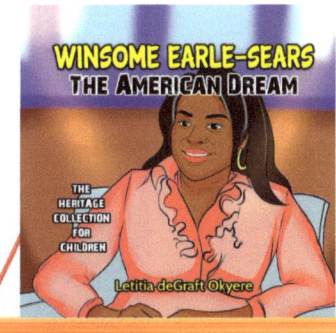 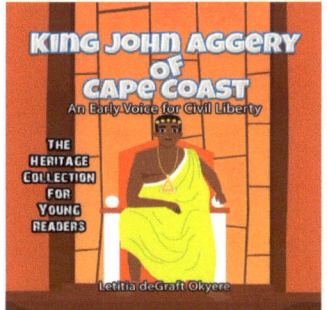 
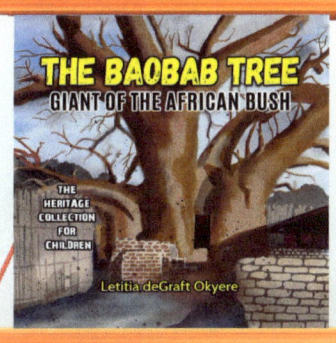 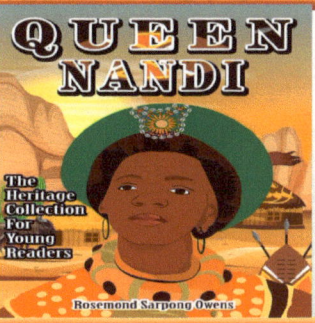 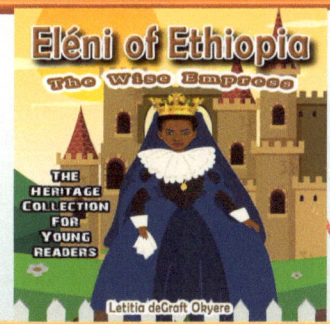
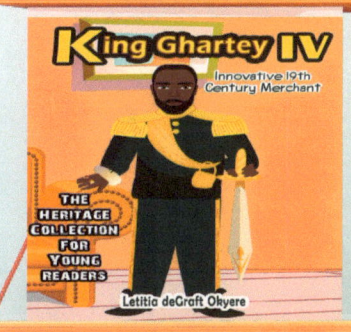 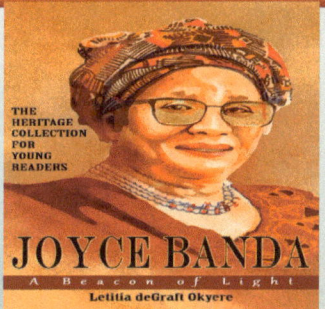 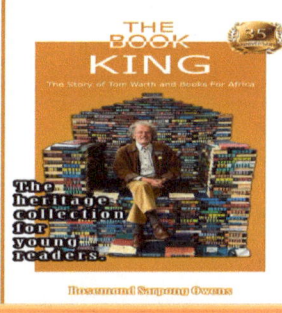
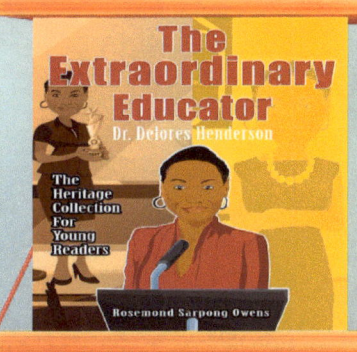 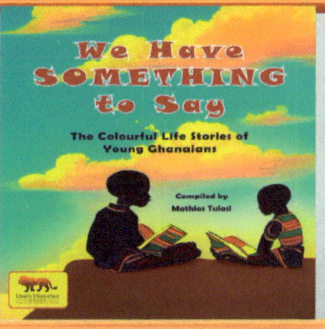 

The End.

www.ingramcontent.com/pod-product-compliance
Lightning Source LLC
Chambersburg PA
CBHW041407010526
44107CB00015B/1098